JUDO
is for me

John Ralph Holm
and Lori Harman

photographs by
Bob and Diane Wolfe

Lerner Publications Company   Minneapolis

The authors would like to thank the University of Minnesota
Judo and Jacket Wrestling Club and team and their friends.

To my mom and dad —J.R.H.

LIBRARY OF CONGRESS CATALOGING-IN-PUBLICATION DATA

Holm, John Ralph.
 Judo is for me.

 (A Sports for me book)
 Summary: A young student of judo discovers how it is
practiced for physical fitness, fun, and self-defense,
and takes part in his first judo contest.
 1. Judo—Juvenile literature. [1. Judo] I. Harman,
Lori. II. Wolfe, Robert L., ill. III. Wolfe, Diane,
ill. IV. Title. V. Series: Sports for me books.
GV114.H65   1986   796.8'152   85-23936
ISBN 0-8225-1149-5 (lib. bdg.)

Manufactured in the United States of America

International Standard Book Number: 0-8225-1149-5
Library of Congress Catalog Card Number: 85-23936

1 2 3 4 5 6 7 8 9 10 95 94 93 92 91 90 89 88 87 86

Hi! My name is Zachariah—or Zach, for short—and I recently discovered the great sport of judo. I had first seen judo on TV when watching the Olympics. Then, one afternoon this summer, I found out that my neighbor Lori was a two-time national judo champion and a teacher of judo at our university.

Lori showed me some of her judo trophies and some photographs of her fighting in judo tournaments. What she was doing in the photos looked so exciting that I began to ask her lots of questions.

Lori told me that judo is a special style of wrestling that is practiced for fun, physical fitness, and competition by boys, girls, men, and women. In an emergency situation, judo can also be an excellent method of self-defense.

In judo, two **players**, or fighters, who are usually of similar weight and ability try to throw or hold down each other. Lori said that *how* a person uses his or her strength is more important than the amount of strength one has. This explains how a small person can throw a large person, a woman can throw a man, or an elderly person can throw a much younger person.

Lori told me that judo was first practiced in Japan in the 1880s. For centuries, Japanese samurai (warriors) had used a fierce, bare-handed method of combat called "jujitsu." In 1882, Jigoro Kano, a young Japanese student of jujitsu, developed a new wrestling sport from jujitsu called "judo."

Kano dropped jujitsu's striking and kicking and dangerous holds but kept its close-quarter wrestling skills such as throws, hold-downs, chokes, and arm-bars that could be used safely. He stressed fair play and taught his students that it was dishonorable to hurt anyone while performing judo techniques.

Today, Lori said, judo is practiced in all parts of the world and, except for 1968, it has been an official men's event in the Olympic Games since 1964. In the future, judo will probably be an Olympic event for women, too. In 1980, the first Women's World Judo Championship was held in Madison Square Garden in New York City.

Later that same day, I asked Lori if she thought I could learn judo. She smiled and said, "Of course," and invited me to a judo class that she helped teach at the university gym. Lori said the T-shirt and sweatpants I was wearing would be fine for practice. I ran home to get permission to go, and Lori drove us to the gym.

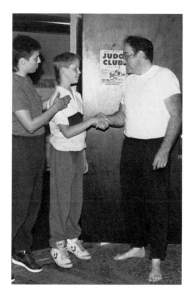

When we arrived, Lori introduced me to her coach, Professor John R. Holm. Coach Holm said he would be happy to have me in his class if I were willing to work hard. I said I was.

Coach Holm told me that many of his students have become state, national, and international judo champions. He said he uses modern teaching methods and equipment, including computers that analyze movement and videotapes of practices and contests. He also emphasizes **biomechanics** —the science of how muscle groups work.

Coach said judo athletes wear a uniform consisting of a loose-fitting jacket, a belt, and ankle-length baggy pants. No shoes or socks are worn. The jacket has several rows of extra stitching along the neckline (collar) to strengthen it because the edge of the jacket is gripped by the opposing judo player during practice and in contests.

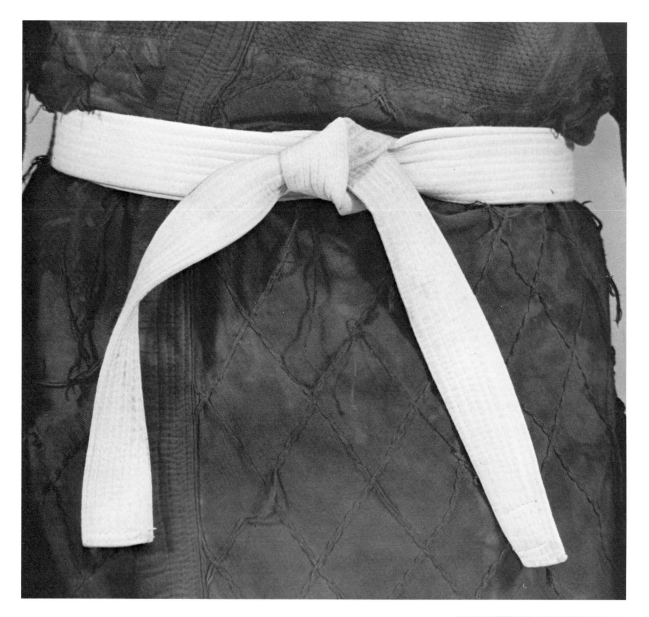

The belt is wrapped around the waist twice and tied in front in a square knot. In some judo clubs, the color of the belt shows how much time a player has spent in judo and his or her general level of ability.

At official judo contests, fighters wear all-white uniforms. I hope to have my own judo uniform someday.

I noticed that other students were doing stretching and warm-up exercises on large mats. Coach Holm said the large, thick mat is built on a special spring-loaded platform to provide extra safety and comfort.

Before learning the beginning throws and hold-downs, Coach Holm said I must first know some safety rules about judo. First of all, we should *never* throw another student who has not been trained to be thrown. Just as important, we should never let anyone throw us until we have learned to fall safely. And throwing and falling should always be practiced on a mat, not on the floor.

In case that medical help is needed, emergency telephone numbers and first-aid supplies should always be handy. At any judo practice or contest, someone should know the first-aid techniques that might be needed for injuries such as sprains, dislocations, fractures, or for unconsciousness.

A special safety feature in judo wrestling is **tapping**, the universal signal for giving up. Tapping two times or more on the mat or on your opponent means you want a hold or an action stopped. An opponent should always respond to a tap immediately. In senior competition, tapping is usually used to end a **submission hold** (advanced choking techniques and armbars), and the player who "taps out" loses the match. Another way to signal giving up is to say "OK," "stop," or "I give."

Coach said another safety rule is to always do warm-up and stretching exercises before practice and contests. Warming up by stretching the neck, back, arms, hands, and legs will help to prevent injuries. Coach Holm and Lori then led the whole class in some warm-ups.

Now I was ready to learn my first throw. Coach Holm showed me the basic position for the **split throw**. He had me jump, turn, and land with my feet wide apart so that my weight was over my toes and my upper body was leaning forward slightly.

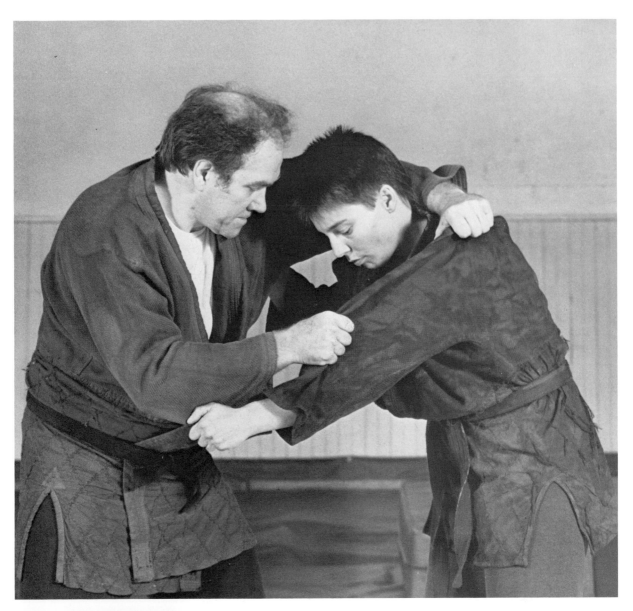

Many techniques, including the split throw, involve grabbing the opponent's uniform, so Coach and Lori showed me how to grab tightly on the sleeve and collar areas. Coach said a good grip is strong but does not make the arms and hands tired. Then Coach asked me to try to grip the collar and sleeve of Lori's uniform.

Next, Lori demonstrated the complete split throw. It was fast and snappy. I watched again very closely as two other students practiced the split throw.

I practiced the throwing position for the split throw five more times. When I had finished, Coach said my form looked good and that I could try the complete throw. When I finally did the throw, I was nervous and a little shaky, but my partner went down easily. It was almost like magic!

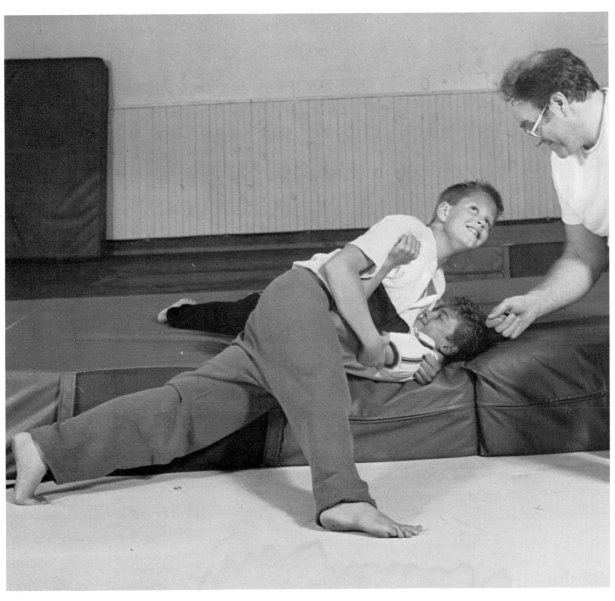

Coach Holm said I should do many **repetitions** (one throw done right after another) and be able to do them while my opponent moved in all directions around the mat. After I did 10 split throws, I thought I would rest a bit. But before I could sit down, Coach asked me to try doing the split throw on the other side.

When I asked Coach to show me how, he said I should first try to figure it out myself. I knew I had to change my grip from the left collar to the right collar and my sleeve grip to the other sleeve. I'd also have to change the position of my feet.

I thought I knew what to do, so I jumped in for the throw. But I jumped the same way as before. My grip was different, but I

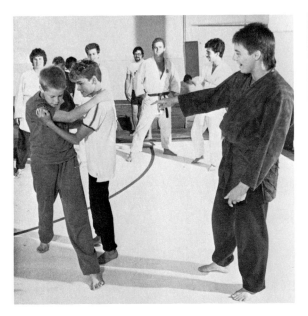

landed with my feet in the same position, so I was all twisted up. It felt funny and must have looked funny, too. Everybody started laughing—even me!

When I tried the throw again, I jumped in correctly and did my first left split throw. I did it over and over. It was fun! After I had done about 25 throws, Coach said I could get a drink of water and rest for a few minutes.

After a short break, we learned another judo technique, the **hold-down**. When using a hold-down in a judo match, it is control that counts and not merely the pinning of the shoulders.

The first hold-down Coach taught was the **smother hold**. You don't actually "smother" your opponent, but you do lay directly on his or her head-and-chest area. Lori demonstrated a smother hold for me. Her opponent was a man much bigger than herself, yet she was able to hold him down for a full 30 seconds! She repeated it one more time, and then Coach showed me how to do it.

First, Coach had me kneel above my partner's head. Then he said I should lay on her chest and be as heavy as I could. Next, he had me grab under my partner's arms, grip the sides of her belt with both hands, and pull in toward myself as tightly as I could. Coach showed me how to keep my legs far apart so that they could brace me strongly and keep me in a position of strength. He

said I should also press my hips down hard.

Coach shouted, "Go!" I tried hard to hold my partner down, but she got away after about 15 seconds. Coach told me to try again but to reposition my legs when my partner struggled to get away. He explained that moving my legs to stay in line with my partner's body when she moved would help my bracing to be stronger.

When I tried the smother hold again, I moved a lot more and tried to keep my legs in line with my partner's body. She could not get away, and I held strong for 30 seconds. Then I tried the smother hold on Lori so she could tell how I was doing. I put the hold-down on her, and she started to struggle around. Suddenly, she was out and away from me—just as though I wasn't even there. Boy, is she fast and tricky!

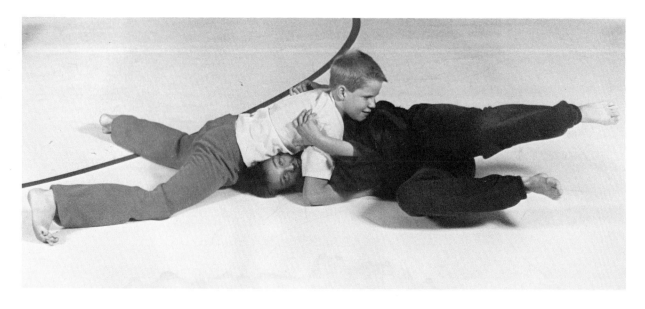

When it was time for the class to end, I didn't want to leave because I was having so much fun. Coach Holm told me to come to class the next day, and he showed me some exercises to practice at home. I said I would be back, and I thanked him for my first lesson. As Lori and I drove home, I thought about all the new skills I had learned.

At the beginning of the next class, Coach Holm told us how well we had done the night before. Then he talked to the beginners about the importance of enthusiasm, dedication, and perseverence in judo. Coach also told us that although we would all be learning the same techniques, each of us would be encouraged to develop his or her own unique style of fighting.

After our warm-ups, we reviewed and
practiced the split throw and the smother
hold while Coach and Lori watched and
helped us. Then we learned another throw,
the **side driver**. It looked similar to the split
throw except that one of Lori's legs hooked
her partner's leg, and she threw him to
his side.

Although the side driver was a **side throw**, and the split throw was a **front throw**, the basic principle was the same for both. The side driver felt a bit different from the split throw, but it was easy to do. I did 25 repetitions on each side, and I was definitely tired when I finished.

Next, Coach Holm taught us a new hold-down, the **arm-and-head hold-down**. Lori demonstrated it on me and told me to try to get away from her, but there was no way. I could barely wiggle my eyeballs! She was just too skillful.

Then I tried the new hold on Jim, a college student who is about my size. Lori showed me how to hold around his head, grab onto his sleeve, and keep my feet apart in a different bracing position.

As soon as Lori said, "Go!" Jim started struggling, but I was still holding him when 30 seconds were up. Lori said I had done a great job.

Coach Holm then called us all together and again reminded us not to let others practice their throws on us until we knew how to manage our bodies and fall safely. He said we should avoid falling on our backs whenever possible because points are scored against such falls in contests.

We first learned to do round-offs, cartwheels, overturns, turnouts, and turnins as

ways to move when off balance or about to fall. While more traditional judo clubs often teach falling on the back first, knowing and using these other ways to move will reduce the chance of losing a match because of landing on your back. They will also keep you in a position to **counterattack**, or move against your opponent. Coach calls these moves "**body management skills.**"

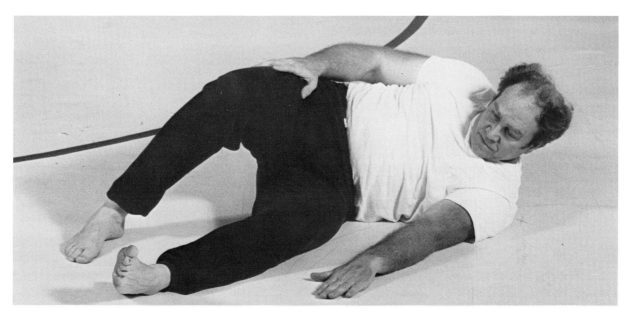

After practicing many of the body management skills, we learned how to fall safely on our sides and backs. Even though back falls should be avoided in contests, they are important to learn because sometimes a throw is so effective that you cannot avoid falling on your back. We use the back fall in practice to give our partner the feeling of a full throw.

Now we were ready for free practice on the mat. In free practice, players try to get their partners in a throw or hold-down while trying not to be taken down themselves. We used the free-practice time to try as many throws and hold-downs as possible, and we changed partners every two minutes. Every judo player has his or her own energy and

style, and it's a challenge to try to outwit and outmaneuver a skilled opponent — especially when he or she is trying to do the same thing to you!

Coach reminded us to keep our movements light and not to smash our partner hard in a throw. Instead, we tried to work together to make a lot of successful moves happen.

At the end of the class, Coach Holm told us about an upcoming judo contest. The contest was to be held in one month and would be a **junior novice tournament** for beginning judo players like myself. Junior contestants are grouped in classes according to age and weight, and the length of each match is usually three minutes with no rest period.

Coach explained that the object of a junior judo match is to win by throwing your opponent down on the mat or by holding him or her on their back or side for a full 30 seconds. Various scores are awarded, depending on the degree of success of a throw or the length of time a hold-down is held.

You win the match instantly if you score a full-point throw or get a hold-down for 30 seconds. If no points are won, the player who came the closest to winning is the winner. In official judo contests, one referee, two judges, a timekeeper, and a scorekeeper are responsible for running the match.

When calling out points for throws and hold-downs and when using international contest terminology, the referee speaks certain words in Japanese. We would be learning the 20 or so Japanese words gradually so that it would be easy.

Coach said any of us were welcome to enter the contest but that those who did should be prepared to attend two-hour practices at least four times a week for the next month. I didn't take long to decide to enter the contest. From the first few practices, I already felt more graceful and lighter on my feet, and I could feel my body getting stronger, too. I felt I could be a winner! Coach and Lori said they would help me to become a skilled and winning fighter.

At our next practice, we learned some additional exercises to strengthen the muscles that are used in judo. First, we were shown the right way to do sit-ups, push-ups, leg sweeps, and weight lifting. Then we did some neck strengthening exercises. These are important for protecting the neck and head.

Coach also had us watch Lori do some advanced skills that we had never seen before. I especially liked her chokes and arm-bars and the way she went from one move into another. I was amazed at her use of power and her trickiness, which Coach Holm called "finesse."

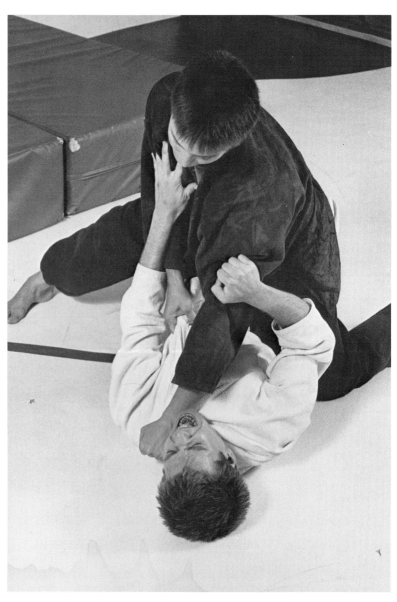

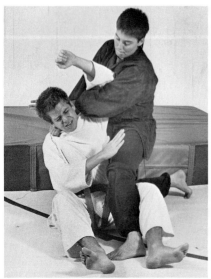

In official competition, a person has to be 13 years old to do the choking techniques and 17 years old to do arm-bars. Coach Holm said that even though I wasn't old enough to use these submission holds in contests, I would be learning them soon. Then, when I was old enough, I would be experienced enough to use them in competition.

As the days went by, Coach and Lori taught me how to do the throws while moving in all directions around the mat—forward, backward, left, and right. Then they showed me how to link my attacks together in case my first one got blocked. We practiced grip fighting, counterthrows, and escapes from hold-downs, and we also worked on flexibility and speed and on ways to fake out an opponent.

We studied an anatomy chart, too. This helped me to understand how warm-up exercises were helping me with my throws and holds. The leg sweeps, for example, help to build up the *gluteus maximus*, or buttocks muscle, which is important for developing powerful throwing skills.

To prepare for the contest, I studied the contest rules almost every day, and I practiced old moves and learned new ones. I wanted to improve faster, but instead my progress seemed to slow down.

When I talked to Lori, she didn't seem surprised and said I was probably in a **"beginner's slump."** She explained that after about three or four weeks of judo training, some students become discouraged because improvement seems slow. The slump is also called a **"learning plateau,"** which is a short period of time when a learner must absorb and understand new skills before they can be fully used. Lori said I should just "stick with it," and soon I would see lots of change for the better.

After that talk, I worked even harder. I tried some more advanced techniques and counterthrows, and I also tried to improve my speed and to move more smoothly. Lori and Coach kept encouraging everyone and said my moves were becoming better every day. The hard work was actually fun, and I began to see results in about a week. I could tell that I was pulling out of the beginner's slump.

During the final weeks before the contest, Coach and Lori reminded me to be sure to get enough sleep, to eat healthy foods, and to cut out extra sweets. They told me not to worry about the moves I still could not do very well. Instead, they said, I should think about the moves I knew the best—and then try to use them at the right time.

Four days before the meet, my parents gave me a wonderful present—my very own judo uniform! I was ready.

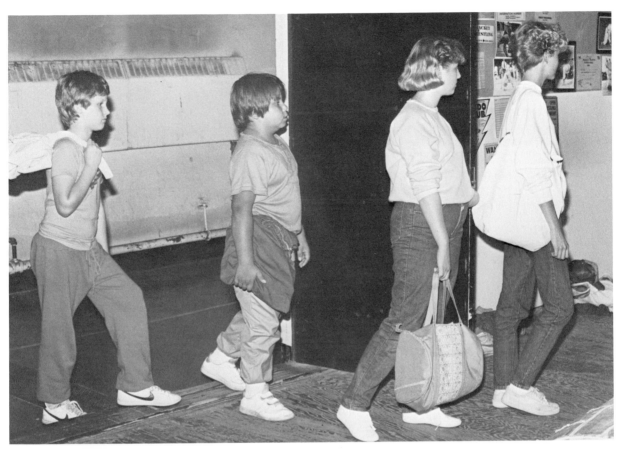

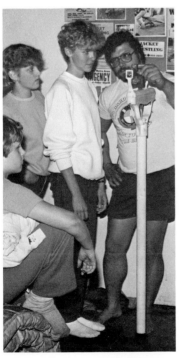

On the day of the contest, I felt great. It was fun to watch all of the new people signing in at our gymnasium. There were three other judo fighters in my weight class, so I knew that I was going to face some real competition.

During the warm-up time, I did cartwheels and round-offs and practiced some of my throws on one of my teammates. Then I heard my name being called on the loud-speaker. The time for my first judo match had arrived.

I went out to the contest area where the referee and the two judges were waiting. When my opponent and I were in position in the center of the mat, the referee gave the command to begin. My opponent reached for me right away, so I took an inside grip around his head.

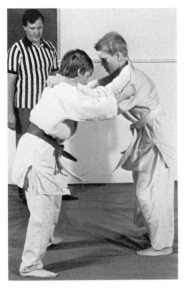

When my opponent stepped to his right, I stepped with him. He stepped again, and this time I did a back-around entry into the split throw. It worked! The referee called, "Ippon!" I had won the match, and it had taken only 11 seconds.

I had a brief rest period while four of my teammates had their fights, and then I was called for my second and final match. This time, I tried another split throw, but it didn't work because my timing was off, and we both fell to the mat. I scrambled really fast, however, and got my opponent into a hold-down.

As soon as the referee saw that I had my opponent under full control, he called out "Osaekomi." That call signaled the timekeeper to begin timing the 30-second hold-down period. My opponent really fought hard to get away, but I managed to hold him for the full 30 seconds. I had won again!

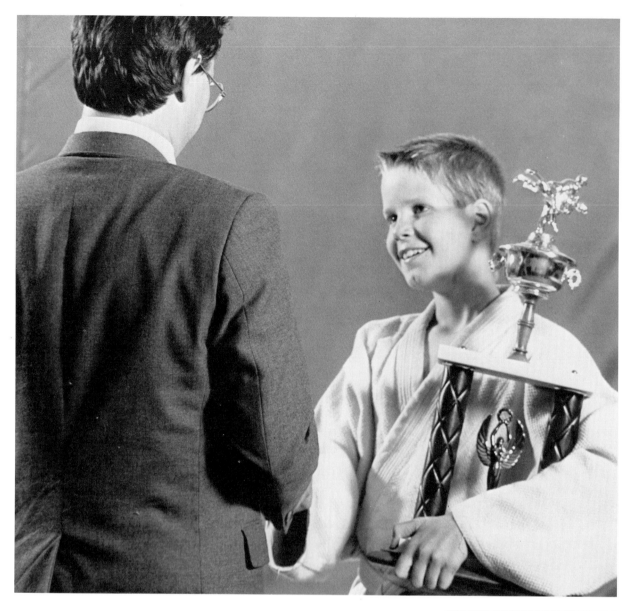

Because I had won my two matches and had no losses, I placed first in my weight division. I received a big trophy—the first of many, I hope. Was I ever happy! Judo is definitely the greatest sport I know. And it's for me!

Words about JUDO

ACTION-REACTION TACTICS: An action that causes an opponent to react in a predictable way

BEGINNER'S SLUMP: A time during which a learner absorbs and understands new skills before being able to fully use them. Although progress is not visible, learning is still taking place. (Also called "learning plateau")

BIOMECHANICS: The science that studies the working of biological, especially muscular, movement

BODY MANAGEMENT SKILLS: The ability to move one's body whenever and wherever one desires; in judo, to use alternative ways of moving such as round-offs and cartwheels instead of falling on the back area

COUNTERATTACK: An attack made to oppose or in response to an opponent's attack

FIGHTER: A person who practices judo (Also called a "player")

FINESSE: Sophisticated movements marked by the use of cleverness and skill

FREE PRACTICE: Paired practice on the mat, during which each player tries to get his or her partner in a throw or hold-down

GLUTEUS MAXIMUS: The buttocks muscle, especially important for powerful throwing

HOLD-DOWN: In judo, the pinning of one's opponent so that his or her general back area touches the mat. In official competition, controlling one's opponent in a hold-down for a full 30 seconds gains a point and wins the match.

JUDO: A style of wrestling in which two players or fighters use knowledge, skill, and timing to try to throw or hold down the other. A jacket is worn in the sport of judo because many moves involve gripping the sleeve, collar, or belt.

JUJITSU: A fierce, bare-handed method of combat used by Japanese warriors in ancient times

LEG SWEEPS: An exercise in which the leg is extended in back to develop the gluteus maximus for more powerful throwing skills

MANEUVER: A skillful method of working, usually involving clever and efficient movements

NOVICE: A person who is new to an activity

REPETITION: The act of performing something again and again

TAPPING: A way for a judo player to signal "I give" by patting his or her opponent or the mat, usually two times or more. Tapping means you want a hold or an action stopped.

ABOUT THE AUTHORS

JOHN R. HOLM has more than 30 years of experience in teaching fighting skills and sports and has taught courses in judo and self defense at the University of Minnesota, Minneapolis, for 20 years. As co-coach of the university's judo and jacket wrestling club and men's and women's team, Holm has developed both national and international champions. Professor Holm, who holds a sixth-degree black belt in judo and a third-degree black belt in jujitsu, is also the creator of the new sport of jacket wrestling, which incorporates techniques and skills from a variety of wrestling sports, including judo.

LORI HARMAN has won seven state judo championships and is a two-time national women's judo champion. She is also a world champion jacket wrestler and is rated number three in the world in women's professional boxing. Co-coach of the judo and jacket wrestling club and team at the University of Minnesota, Harman holds black belt rankings in both judo and jujitsu.